LET'S ROCK!

EXPLORING
EARTH'S
MINERALS

MARIE ROGERS

PowerKiDS
press

New York

Published in 2022 by The Rosen Publishing Group, Inc.
29 East 21st Street, New York, NY 10010

First Edition

Portions of this work were originally authored by Maria Nelson and published as *Earth's Minerals*. All new material this edition authored by Marie Rogers.

Editor: Amanda Vink
Cover Designer: Alan Sliwinski
Interior Designer: Rachel Rising

Photo Credits: Cover, Cagla Acikgoz/Shutterstock.com; Cover, pp. 1, 3, 4, 5, 6, 8, 10, 11, 12, 13, 14, 15, 16, 18, 20, 22, 23, 24, (background) Alex Konon/Shutterstock.com; p. 4 Manutsawee Buapet/Shutterstock.com; p. 5 bogdandimages/Shutterstock.com; p. 6 Madlen/Shutterstock.com; p.7 Jim Barber/Shutterstock.com; p. 9 ShadeDesign/Shutterstock.com; p. 11 Rachmo/Shutterstock.com; pp. 12, 16 Sebastian Janicki/Shutterstock.com; p. 13 Panayot Savov/Shutterstock.com; p.15 antoni halim/Shutterstock.com; pp. 15, 18 Fokin Oleg/Shutterstock.com; p. 17 Mitand73/Shutterstock.com; p. 19 psamtik/Shutterstock.com; p. 20 motah/Shutterstock.com; p. 21 feedbackstudio/Shutterstock.com; p. 22 wawritto/Shutterstock.com.

Some of the images in this book illustrate individuals who are models. The depictions do not imply actual situations or events.

Library of Congress Cataloging-in-Publication Data

Names: Rogers, Marie, 1990- author.
Title: Exploring earth's minerals / Marie Rogers.
Description: New York : PowerKids Press, [2022] | Series: Let's rock! |
    Includes bibliographical references and index.
Identifiers: LCCN 2019051206 | ISBN 9781725319134 (paperback) | ISBN
    9781725319158 (library binding) | ISBN 9781725319141 (6 pack)
Subjects: LCSH: Minerals–Juvenile literature. | Earth (Planet)–Juvenile
    literature.
Classification: LCC QE365.2 .R66 2022 | DDC 549–dc23
LC record available at https://lccn.loc.gov/2019051206

Manufactured in the United States of America

CPSIA Compliance Information: Batch #CWPK22. For further information contact Rosen Publishing, New York, New York at 1-800-237-9932.

Find us on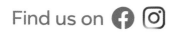

CONTENTS

MANY MINERALS

Diamonds and salt may look different, but they have a lot in common. They're both minerals! Minerals are the building blocks of rocks. They're inorganic, which means they're not made from living or formerly living matter, and they're created naturally. Minerals form underground, and sometimes that can take billions of years. There are more than 4,000 different minerals found on Earth!

Minerals are homogeneous, which means each one has the same chemical makeup throughout. Wherever a mineral is found, its structure always looks the same as other examples of that mineral. If you break up a mineral, its **physical properties** won't change.

DIAMOND ▶

ROCKING OUT

Minerals can be part of rocks, but they're not rocks. A rock is made of one or more minerals, and rocks may also include organic remains. Rocks don't always have the same makeup—they can be made of different things.

SALT ▷

Some minerals, such as salt, are very common. Others, such as diamonds, are rare!

MAKING A MINERAL

Minerals form when the atoms of one or more elements come together and start growing crystals. There are several ways this can happen.

Some minerals form when melted rock from deep within Earth rises to the surface and cools. Others form when weather, especially involving wind and water, wears down rock and causes matter to settle and harden into new forms. Some minerals form when water **evaporates** and substances that have **dissolved** in the water come together. Some minerals are even produced by living things! For example, an oyster produces a mineral called calcite, which makes up its shell.

CALCITE ▶

Oyster pearls aren't minerals. They're a **composite** of the mineral aragonite and the organic compound called conchiolin. An organic compound contains the element carbon and one or more other elements.

7

ATOMS

Each kind of mineral has a makeup that's different than every other kind of mineral. Scientists can figure out the elements that make up minerals by observing their atoms. The atoms of each element are arranged in a special repeating pattern.

"Atom" is the general term for one of the smallest units of matter. Atoms are made of electrically charged particles, or very small pieces of something. Particles with the same electric charges **repel** each other, and particles that have different electric charges **attract** each other. These particles say what the atom, the elements, and the minerals will look like.

The first atoms were primarily hydrogen and helium. These elements are still some of the most widely found in the universe.

THE STRUCTURE OF AN ATOM

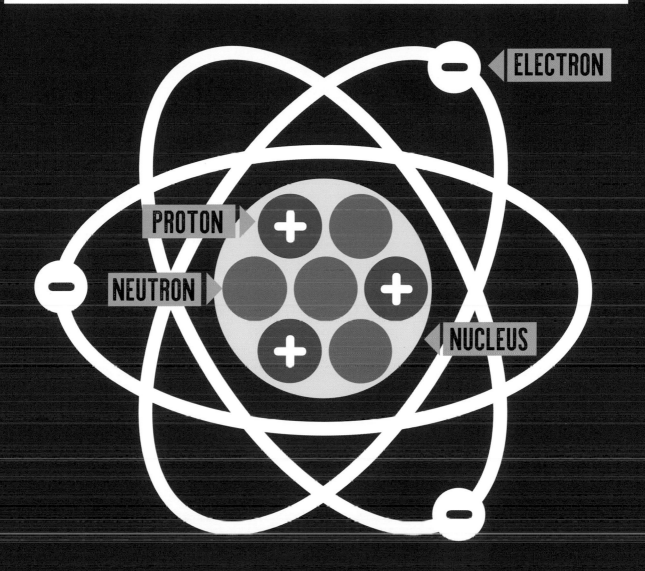

ELECTRON

PROTON

NEUTRON

NUCLEUS

Nucleus: The center of an atom.

Neutron: A particle without an electric charge.

Proton: A particle with a positive electric charge.

Electron: A particle with a **negative** charge.

CRYSTALS!

Minerals can be beautiful. They come in many colors and shapes. Mineral crystals grow and branch out underground. Their atoms lock into place in a pattern that creates the same shape over and over, often producing cubes and snowflake patterns. Sometimes, minerals don't have room to grow in these shapes, so they crash into one another and form large **conglomerated** masses. This type of mineral can be harder to recognize.

Many mineral crystals take thousands of years to fully form. Salt, however, can grow crystals quickly. Sometimes it just takes a few hours for salt crystals to fully form!

Some minerals have different colors because of impurities, or low concentrations of other elements. For example, beryl, a mineral, is green if it contains a small amount of chromium. That makes it an emerald!

ROCKING OUT

In labs, scientists can make minerals that are almost exactly the same as those that form naturally. However, since they didn't form in nature, these aren't true minerals. Minerals such as **gemstones** that are grown in labs don't increase in value the way the ones found in nature do. That's because more can always be made in the future.

Sometimes identifying a mineral is as simple as looking at it. People who study and collect minerals can often tell a mineral's type by simple observations. They might look at the color and the size of the mineral's crystals, for example.

Another recognizable feature of a mineral is its transparency, or how much light shines through it. For example, you can often see through rock crystal, a common type of quartz. A mineral's **luster** is noticeable, too. Minerals can be said to be metallic or nonmetallic. Lead, for example, can be metallic before it's exposed to oxygen in the air. Then it rusts.

QUARTZ ▶

ROCKING OUT

Scientists put minerals in groups to make them easier to identify. The minerals in each group have similarities to each other. Some mineralogists, or people who study minerals, divide minerals up by their crystal structures. There are seven major chemical groups.

We now know that lead can be toxic. People often replace old household things that have lead in them, including paint and pipes.

WHEN MINERALS BREAK

Other physical properties help people tell minerals apart. We can measure how hard minerals are. All minerals fall somewhere on a hardness scale. Scientists may also look at a mineral's streak, which is the color of the mineral when it's rubbed on something else.

When some minerals break, they crack along weaker areas in smooth planes and form certain shapes. Diamonds, for example, often break in an octahedral shape, which is a shape with eight nearly equal faces. How minerals tend to break along flat surfaces is called cleavage. Other minerals don't have these weak planes, and they don't break in a regular fashion. When minerals tend to do this, it's called fracture.

ROCKING OUT

The Mohs' scale of mineral hardness orders minerals from 1—the softest minerals—to 10. The higher a mineral's number on the scale, the fewer other minerals can scratch it. This scale was developed by a German mineralogist named Friedrich Mohs in 1812.

Some people become professional gemstone cutters. These people use knowledge about a mineral's cleavage and fracture to cut the most valuable gems.

FRACTURE

CLEAVAGE

COLOR

Some minerals are the same color both from piece to piece and throughout a single piece. However, some can be many colors. This may be because of the presence of a small amount of an element, such as the iron that makes quartz turn purple. The quartz is then amethyst!

Since mineral color can also change with strong heat or light, it's not a perfect way to identify minerals. Some minerals are part of a series. That means their structure is mostly the same, but the elements in them differ slightly. In these instances, the minerals may share many of the same **characteristics**—including color!

QUARTZ

While minerals within a series can be very similar, they can also be different colors!

PHYSICAL PROPERTIES

Scientists can also measure the specific gravity of a mineral. That's the relative weight of the mineral to an equal volume of water. Because there are so many minerals, it can be hard to tell them apart. Scientists may look for other **distinguishing** features. Does the mineral in question taste of anything? Does the mineral shine **fluorescent** under a black light? Does it smell like anything?

These physical properties are important in identifying a mineral because different minerals can be made of the same elements. For example, the element carbon makes up both very hard diamonds and very soft graphite.

GRAPHITE ▶

Quartz is one of the most common minerals on Earth.

MADE FROM MINERALS

Humans use Earth's minerals for many things! We use quartz to make glass. We use copper to make wires and computer chips. We use limestone, aluminum, and many other minerals for building. People sometimes make airplanes out of titanium. Many minerals are worth a lot of money, either because they're useful or because they're hard to find. Others are cheaper and plentiful. For example, gypsum is used to make drywall, which people use to build walls inside some homes.

Jewelry is made from minerals. Gold and silver are commonly made into rings, earrings, and necklaces. Some pieces also feature gemstones—which are cut and polished minerals!

People used to think that diamond was the hardest mineral. Now we know there may be some harder mincrals, but they're very rare.

21

WE NEED MINERALS!

People can find minerals in many places since they form all over the world in different conditions. Many people like to collect them! Years ago, collectors searched mines for minerals. Today, however, only workers or mine owners are allowed into most mines. There are large international mineral shows that happen every year, and this gives collectors and sellers a chance to get together. Minerals are also on display at many museums.

We also need some minerals in order to survive. These minerals, including calcium, potassium, and sodium, are naturally found in many foods. Sodium chloride, which contains sodium, is also commonly known as table salt!

GLOSSARY

attract: To cause something to go toward something else.

characteristic: A special quality that makes a person, thing, or group different from others.

composite: Made of different parts or elements.

conglomerate: Made up of a bunch of pieces gathered together into a whole.

dissolve: To break down a solid when it's mixed with a liquid.

distinguish: To recognize one thing from others by some mark or quality.

evaporate: To change from a liquid into a gas.

fluorescent: Brilliantly colored and emitting light during or after exposure to electromagnetic waves, such as light.

gemstone: A stone or other matter used in jewelry when cut and polished.

jewelry: Decorative things, such as necklaces and earrings, that people wear on their body.

luster: How shiny a surface is.

negative: Marked by the absence of something.

physical property: Any property that's measurable and able to be observed.

repel: To push away.

INDEX

WEBSITES

Due to the changing nature of Internet links, PowerKids Press has developed an online list of websites related to the subject of this book. This site is updated regularly. Please use this link to access the list:
www.powerkidslinks.com/letsrock/minerals